ECKANKAR

KEY TO PAST LIVES

HAROLD KLEMP

ECKANKAR
Minneapolis
Eckankar.org

ECKANKAR—Key to Past Lives

Copyright © 2003, 2022 ECKANKAR

Printed in USA

Photo of Sri Harold Klemp by Art Galbraith

ISBN: 978-1-57043-562-1

Library of Congress Cataloging-in-Publication Data

Names: Klemp, Harold, author. | Klemp, Harold Past lives, dreams, and soul travel.

Title: Eckankar : key to past lives / Harold Klemp.

Description: Minneapolis : Eckankar, 2024. | "This book has been excerpted from Past Lives, Dreams, and Soul Travel by Harold Klemp, copyright ©2003 Eckankar"-- T.p. verso. | Summary: "Author Harold Klemp, spiritual leader of Eckankar, offers stories of inspiration to help you on your own journey home to God. Bring more harmony to your life by untangling karmic webs from long ago"-- Provided by publisher.

Identifiers: LCCN 2024010185 | ISBN 9781570435621 (paperback)

Subjects: LCSH: Eckankar (Organization) | Reincarnation.

Classification: LCC BP605.E3 K55366 2024 | DDC 299/.93--dc23/eng/20240414

LC record available at https://lccn.loc.gov/2024010185

♾ This paper meets the requirements of ANSI/NISO Z39.48-1992 (Permanence of Paper).

Contents

Introduction

$\mathscr{B}$esides the many tips and insights, the stories in this book are accounts of God's people doing godly things.

Past lives, along with dreams and Soul Travel, are of great importance to the spiritual life. A true knowledge and practice of them leads to the most satisfying and fulfilling life you could ever imagine—or wish for.

And here it is, the inspiration to help you on your own journey to God.

How does the Holy Spirit, the ECK, relate to us? Read these stories, and learn of many ways in which God talks to people. What does God say? Are the divine messages of universal reach, or are they love whisperings for us alone?

1

And why does God speak?

Read the stories in this book, and you'll find many answers to questions of your own. The stories come from every walk of life. They were chosen with you in mind.

Today is a special time in the history of mankind. It is now possible to tell of past lives without fear of censure, persecution, or worse. A window of opportunity is open. It has opened for you.

What makes a spiritual life? Read and see. Do you want freedom, knowledge, truth, or wisdom? Love?

Look no further. The passkey is in your hands. Feel free to use it.

1
You Have
Lived Before

$\mathcal{A}$ six-year-old boy was seated near me, next to the window on an airplane flying over Louisiana. Looking down at the vast marshland with its many intersecting channels of water, he turned to his mother and called out in an excited voice, "It looks just like Ethiopia."

The embarrassed mother tried to quiet him. Everybody knows that Ethiopia isn't in the middle of a marsh, because drought has drained life from the place.

A businessman, sitting across the aisle from the boy, lowered his newspaper and began to chuckle. "Ethiopia!" he said. "Have you ever been to Ethiopia, boy?" He laughed, relishing the thought of any likeness at all between Ethiopia and Louisiana.

"It looks like Ethiopia," the boy said.

The man erupted into a bellow of laughter. Other passengers joined in. "The boy thinks Louisiana looks like Ethiopia," he said, repeating the boy's words for anyone who might have missed them. This brought a fresh peal of laughter.

The chastened boy grew quiet, and his mother flushed a bright red. When the plane was ready to land, the boy said to her, "We're almost there."

"Where?" his mother asked.

The boy hesitated. Rather than say, "Ethiopia," he said, "There!"

The boy had recalled a distant past when certain areas of the world, now dry and brown, had enjoyed lush vegetation. His memory of those days was clear and certain. He remembered the past, because he had caught a glimpse from a higher spiritual vantage point. His eyes had glimpsed the Time Track.

Wheel of Reincarnation

Most people on earth are returnees. They've been here before, and they'll return another time. The term for this recycling of lifetimes is the wheel of reincarnation. Karma, people's action and reaction in life, is its motor. The cycle goes on—lifetime after lifetime.

People of the Christian faith believe that when one dies, that's it. One life, one time, and then heaven or hell. They don't recognize the unchanging Law of Karma that nonetheless plucks them back to earth. They're on the Wheel of the Eighty-Four, a reference to the many thousands of lives that people enter in the lower worlds of matter, energy, space, and time.

It's a very dreary cycle. After a person recycles through many successive lives, a feeling comes that something's amiss with this scene, that something's wrong with the script. Then a thought creeps in. He begins to wonder about the "one life, one time" theory. Could it be in error?

He begins to grope for the truth.

It is common in today's media to come across some direct or indirect references to reincarnation. Some of the stories give a clear insight into it.

Yet how easy it is to dismiss a past-life story with, "Just another dreamer's tall tale." And it's a real temptation to discredit young children who give detailed accounts of past lifetimes. Even if it means ignoring the candid descriptions of settings, situations, and possible family ties of old. Yet this happens all the time in families with children up to five or six years of age. Take, for example, the boy on the plane, who recalled the Ethiopia of a greener age.

It's hard for some people in a Christian society to accept this information about reincarnation as a foundation for the miracle of birth. So they make up other explanations, that past-life claims are maybe some kind of mental transference. But wouldn't it be less of a problem to accept the simple fact of rebirth? Then you'd find sense behind the bounds of reincarnation.

Genius and disability are two quick examples of the influence of past lives.

People of religions other than ECKANKAR know and accept the principle of reincarnation. It's a principle of divine love in action.

Reincarnation allows people, like you and me, to have a chance to develop the quality of divine love. This opportunity comes through the hardships and uncertainties of life, as well as in the joys and fulfillment of living. So we develop the quality of divine love.

This love makes us more godlike beings.

AWAKENING YOUR PAST LIVES

If you want a look at your past lives, the word to sing for a few minutes at bedtime is *Mana* (say MAH-nah). Then go to sleep as usual. This word attunes you with the Causal Plane, the region of past-life memories. Remembering past lives takes practice. But others do it, and so can you.

Our Spiritual
Wake-Up Calls

Soul, when It came to earth this time, made an agreement with Itself to reach some goal and thus make headway in spiritual unfoldment.

Back in the 1930s, during the Depression, in a slum in Birmingham, England, a young girl of five set off for school. Let's call her Rose. She'd gone to meet her cousin, who would be excused from classes within the hour. All of a sudden, a golden light enfolded her. This golden circle of light was a spiritual wake-up call, and its glory sealed Rose off from the rest of the outside world. She could neither hear nor see others. But, secure in the bliss of the moment, she rested content in the heart of this beautiful golden light.

Imagine a five-year-old child trying to gather words to relate an event of this sort. What adult would have given her two minutes? A celestial light of a half hour's duration that put all surroundings outside the realm of sight or sound? Go run and play, child.

You can see the difficulty. After a few such attempts to tell of the experience, Rose gave up.

Years later Rose decided to learn the nature of her youthful adventure. Thus began diligent research into past lives. By her midthirties, she had been an eager student of both Edgar Cayce and the Rosicrucians. She recalled ads in *Fate* magazine on ECKANKAR. Yet the search went on. She also studied Astara and Theosophy and read the books of H. Rider Haggard and others.

In 1972, Rose was startled by sightings of UFOs.

Along the way she'd become a devotee of three different branches of Buddhism. In quick succession came marriage to an executive in the movie industry and a family of three children. Rose also kept a busy social calendar. A fast-paced life, indeed.

Her agreement with herself from before this lifetime was on this order: to make a broad and thorough study of world religions and psychic groups. So she read books on every subject. In time, she gained a solid knowledge about the variety of ideas on truth.

Soul begins each lifetime with a clean slate.

The Lords of Karma erase memory of an individual's old mistakes, which allows for a fresh start. This kindness sidesteps a dead end. It avoids the error of someone taking up a new life and wasting it on past-life problems like revenge for a lost love, property, or social position.

Such memory loss is thus of benefit to Soul's progress. Then, somewhere along the line, Divine Spirit sends a spiritual wake-up call through one means or another.

The message is, "OK, it's time to remember why you came to earth."

Of course, the memory of one's spiritual mission is seldom relayed in such clear speech. Many go through years of doubt and uncertainty. They sample one religion or another, tripping from area to area in the occult field, or shifting from philosophy to psychology, even to mathematics. It's all in pursuit of the key to life and truth.

Sometimes a seeker makes few apparent gains but at some point says, "There's got to be more than this."

Some inner nudge leaves him unhappy with the knowledge so far gained. Some hidden impulse of the heart drives him on in unending pursuit of God and truth.

Coming Back

We used to have lots of cats on the farm. Every so many years there were three new kittens: one with gray-and-white patches, another with black-and-white spots, and a striped tiger kitten. Farm life was an unforgiving one, so they often translated (died) within a couple of years. Soon after, though, the same little group of three kittens came back in a new litter. Soul took a kitty's body until that body wore out. It would then leave for a while and sometime later return in a new cat body.

12

The same principle of reincarnation holds in the case of family and friends who die and pass on. It's common to feel sadness at the loss—it's natural. But when Soul can pass into a higher state of consciousness, into a more joyful world, It discovers a happiness that outshines every dream. It is content in Its new state.

I Knew You When You Were Old

A young girl accompanied her father to a retirement home to visit a great aunt. Arriving at the relative's room, they met the great aunt's roommate for the first time. Her name was Sophie. She was well along in years and close enough to the other side of life to catch a glimpse of life in those exalted places. Yet when she spoke of it to others, people shook their heads in resignation.

"Poor old Sophie," they said. "She's lost her mind."

The young girl walked into the room, passed by her great aunt, and headed straight for old Sophie. The two studied each other for a long time. Breaking the silence, Sophie, in a low voice, said, "I know you. I knew you when you were an old lady."

The little girl's clear gaze searched the woman. The look on the child's face said it, too, held a memory. "I knew you when you were a young lady," said the girl.

Two old friends touching bases.

The great aunt approached from across the room and patted her grandniece on the arm. "Don't mind Sophie," she said. "Her mind likes to wander."

How easy it is for someone in the dark about reincarnation to discredit the wisdom of both age and youth.

WHAT PULLS YOU?

An attraction, say, to knights, medieval wars, and battles could be from a faint memory of past lives in some period of history. A Civil War buff, no doubt, saw military service during the tumultuous 1860s. That war left such a scar on the American nation that it still reveals itself as a deeply felt interest in Civil War history.

A child with a passion for model airplanes might have flown as an aviator in World War I or II, or even as a starship commander from Atlantis.

Someone with a feeling of ill will toward a certain church or country for no apparent reason may once have been a victim of religious or political fervor. An ailment without a known cause, such as a chronic neck pain, may be a tip-off that a person was once hanged or beheaded.

Whenever strong loves or hates appear with no seeming cause, it means we are drawing the past into the present by agreement.

Between Lifetimes

Anyone in harmony with the true way of the Holy Spirit will demonstrate the survival factor. It means doing whatever it takes to survive another day. Why make the effort? Because every second of life is a precious moment. Each day offers another chance to learn more about God's love.

Soul, at some point, will return to a new life on earth. No matter how hard Soul finds life, earth is an excellent place to learn the many dimensions of divine love.

Not just in the receiving of love, but in the giving of it.

* * *

The next two stories come from Earth to God, Come In Please . . . , *books 1 and 2. They offer a unique insight into occasions in which the ECK, Divine Spirit, gave ordinary people an extraordinary insight into truth. Read these accounts for a closer look at the miracles of life.*

Checkers

By Doug Culliford

One child was six, and the other three. It was a preholiday gathering of family, and someone popped the question:

"What do you want for Christmas?"

"Checkers," replied the six-year-old girl. "I want checkers for Christmas."

"Checkers! Why, you don't even know how to play the game."

"Yes, I do!" the little girl said.

"Who taught you how to play checkers? Did you learn in school? Did your parents teach you?"

"Nobody did. We always used to play checkers." The girl's eyes were mirrors of truth.

"You and who else?" someone asked.

"My brother and I." The three-year-old brother looked up and nodded agreement to the questioning adults. "We used to play before, when we were big."

"Before? When was that?"

"When we were big before. Before we came to live here. We were old, older than you."

One adult consulted another. Minutes later, someone found an old, dusty box of checkers and set them up in front of the two children. Sure enough, the moves were familiar to them. They played like old hands. The adults looked on in bewilderment as the boy and girl nimbly moved pieces around the board.

"Did you live together before?" someone asked.

The little boy kept on playing, letting his older sister do the talking. "My brother and I lived in the same house then. We were married."

Someone mentioned a deceased uncle.

The little girl piped up, "I knew him too! I met him before I came here to live with you!"

This uncle had died before the six-year-old was born, and the doubting adults shook their heads at her fantasy.

But she went on to describe him in perfect detail.

Now comes a curious thing. This family held to a particular religion that didn't acknowledge reincarnation. But over the years they had had many mysterious encounters with deceased relatives until, bit by bit, the family crossed the fine line between religious doctrine and actual spiritual experience. They began to acknowledge through the certainty of these experiences that reincarnation was not only possible, but probable.

And so they moved one step further from their limitations and a step closer to spiritual freedom.

Halloween Surprise

By Cameron Fox

The Halloween committee met every week for six weeks to plan the party for the hospital employees. We wanted everyone to have plenty of time to decide upon their costumes.

Many of the hospital jobs revolve around crisis intervention and other stressful life-and-death situations.

These parties are a time when all departments can share their lunch hour, dress up in bizarre costumes, laugh, and regain a playful, childlike spirit.

The music began promptly at eleven o'clock on the day of the party. Several committee members placed baked goods on the table to be judged. Then the judges—the hospital director, the dietitian, the chaplain, and others—went from item to item tasting the delicious-looking foods.

Hospital employees started coming in—many more than we had expected. The room soon filled with laughing people dressed in costume. This year the costumes were especially creative. One person, dressed as a bag of dirty clothes, had so many rags covering him no one could guess who he was.

After prizes were awarded for the baking contest, the judges took their places in chairs so they could see the contestants in costume as they walked across the stage.

The room was crowded with contestants, committee members, and other members of the hospital staff. All eyes were on the stage. One by one, contestants began to walk slowly across it, and some performed a skit to go along with the costume. Raggedy Ann did a short dance, the rock singer sang for us, and the soldier marched.

Finding a comfortable place to sit toward the back of the room, I closed my eyes for a moment and began a silent chant of HU, another name for God.

Singing this love song to God is something I often do. It gives a sense of peace and purpose, and lessens anxiety during a busy or stressful day.

After chanting for a few moments, I opened my eyes and gazed around the room. I had the feeling this might be a dream. Yet, looking down at my Gypsy costume, I knew it was not. I had dressed as a Gypsy every Halloween for years. As a child I had even performed in a chorus of Gypsy dancers for a ballet recital.

Closing my eyes a moment, I saw a vivid picture. It was much like a picture postcard. There appeared a vision of me dancing around a fire with others dressed like Gypsies.

By choosing this outfit again and again, I was stepping back to a time in the eleventh century when I was learning lessons of survival as a Gypsy.

Many times in my job as a counselor I am called on to assist patients to find meaning in their lives. This requires teaching basic survival skills such as physical, mental, and environmental health. As a counselor, I am often among highly emotional, even unpredictable people. This does not upset me.

I learned survival skills and an ability to balance uncertainties during that Gypsy lifetime. They continue to be useful to me even today.

Sitting in the back of the room, I felt as if I were surrounded by light. That light projected to five other co-workers in the room—the gorilla, the pilgrim, the cat, the Indian, and the soldier. Of all the costumed workers, these were the most comfortable and believable in their roles.

Had they chosen their costumes for the same reason I had chosen mine—for the chance to step back into the past?

When these contestants took their turns upon the stage, everyone in the room applauded. The judges, too, were obviously impressed. These five were each awarded the top prize—dinner for two at the best restaurant in town.

Halloween has taken on a whole new meaning! It will never be quite the same for me again.

2
Past Lives, Present Lessons

$\mathcal{O}$dd as it may seem, you had a special reason for coming into this lifetime. It was to become a more godlike being, but most people do not realize this fact. They assume that birth is a fancy of destiny.

I'm here; I don't know why, they think. *Bad luck, maybe? Troublesome place, this.*

All in all, earth is nothing other than a spiritual school. God designed and set up this place so that you and every other Soul here may develop godlike qualities and thus become more like God.

Many people think they exist to fill time and space until the trumpets sound on that last day. Then, having lived a fruitless, selfish life, they expect to fly to some higher world, to continue a useless, self-serving life there as well.

Not so, me hearties.

No, indeed. The purpose of life is to become a Coworker with God. It means service to others, using our talents and interests to give hand, ear, or heart to another in need.

All the lives you have ever lived were for the polishing of Soul. Like it or not, you are now at a higher and more spiritual level than in any prior incarnation. So look at yourself. Do you like what you see? Keep in mind, whatever it is, for better or worse, it's of your own making.

You are the sum of all your thoughts, feelings, and actions from this life and every lifetime in the past.

Past Lives
Are Tied to Karma

Sometimes people ask, "What does ECKANKAR have to offer that's unique? How

26

is it different from Christianity?" So I may speak to them of karma and reincarnation.

People, in general, think of karma as an unpleasant force and less often as having a beneficial side. Take for example Mozart, already composing music at age five.

The rule of karma determines factors like male or female body, eye-hand coordination, long- or short-term memory retention, and desires. In addition, our karmic package includes race, ancestry, family, friends, economic and social standing, and much more besides.

However, what comes of those conditions depends upon the exercise of our free will.

The Law of Cause and Effect, or the Law of Karma, is always in play your whole life. You must know how to live in harmony with its exacting terms. The experiences that derive from an adolescent or mature understanding of that law will, in time, bring you to an acceptance of divine love. That's the reason you're here.

Family Karmic Groups

In the 1890s, a young girl and her six brothers and sisters came by ship from Europe to America. A fever struck during the voyage across the Atlantic. It cost the lives of her siblings. All were lost.

This girl arrived in America, grew up, and later married. She had six children. These returning Souls were the brothers and sisters who had perished on the voyage from Europe. Being such a tight-knit karmic group, they kept incarnating with each other.

Years later, one of these children died in an accident. He reincarnated four months later as the son of one of her other children. Many noted the boy's resemblance to his deceased uncle. When the boy grew to manhood, he stayed around the family home, doing repairs and taking care of the family members as he had before as the uncle.

Only two of the six children in this woman's family ever married. Since they were such a close karmic group, most of them preferred each other's company to that of others.

When these Souls find ECKANKAR, this family karma will begin to melt. They will work through traits and conditions that have bound them to each other for many lives, and so again move on in their spiritual lives. Karma may create a net of fear. These Souls carried a fear of life, the reason for the inseparable bond that stretched back for centuries.

Yet when love appears, fear must flee; love brings freedom.

Good and Bad Karma

People like to think of karma as bad. Yet there's a balance between the good and bad; it's the way of spiritual law. Overall there is as much good karma as bad—but one or the other enjoys dominance at a time.

For this reason some people are without a home. Others bask in wealth. A homeless person may be selfish or generous, while the same traits hold for a wealthy individual.

This example suggests a tension between the making and dissolving of good and bad karma.

The scale of divine justice weighs all karma. Its measure is exact. Every thought, word, and deed stands naked in the court of divine judgment.

Insight into Another Life

A group of students from Ghana traveled to another country for a year's study. They wanted to become more fluent in French.

One of the girls, a black student, happened to meet a white German man. Soon they were close friends. Her acquaintances started to talk.

"Got a romance going?" they asked. "With a whitey?"

When someone of a different race, nationality, or even habits breaches the established order of a community, many times it's a recipe for trouble. Eyebrows are raised, and fair-weather friends run up their true colors. So her friends began to spread rumors and pass falsehoods about her friendship with this white German male. The girl wished to lose neither her friends from Ghana nor her new white companion.

She debated about the best course to take. To soothe the ferment, she sought counsel in a spiritual exercise.

It's easy to do a spiritual exercise. Shut your eyes and imagine a conversation with your spiritual guide, whomever you feel comfortable sharing the secrets of your heart with. It can be Jesus or some other religious figure. ECKists look to the MAHANTA, the Living ECK Master, the spiritual leader of ECKANKAR.

So in a spiritual exercise, this young woman said, "Please, MAHANTA, give me an insight into this. What can I do? I don't want to lose my friends on this side or my friend on that side."

Such was the concern she laid before the MAHANTA.

In the next instant she became aware of being in a past lifetime, standing on a shore with a baby in her arms. Close off-shore stood a slaving ship. White men dotted the beach. They brandished whips at a line of black slaves ranged along the sand, shackled in chains.

A point of interest: news media report cases of one race accusing another of atrocities. Cruel and inhuman treatment is the charge.

Yet many black people once sold into slavery in Africa were prisoners of war of another black tribe. The conquering tribe had a choice. It could either kill the defeated warriors or trade them for money or goods. In spite of the heartless nature of the choice, it did forestall an immediate death.

Their captors thus delivered them from the interior of the continent where the white men were loath to venture because of malaria and other diseases.

In sum, the fighting between black tribes took place inland. Then the victors marched the captives out and sold them to slavers, who shipped the unfortunate Souls to ports in North or South America. Those voyages saw the most brutal conditions one can imagine.

But revisionists want to rewrite the historical record. Years later, they alter history after the backdrop of those times has been forgotten. Agitators, they twist events to fit a modern personal or political fad. One claim is that all atrocities were the fault of only one party to the action.

Such a revision of history is meant to deceive. It foments new strife.

In this woman's past-life experience, white men herded blacks onto the ships while she watched in tears, with a child at her breast. Her husband was one of the slaves. She begged the slave masters, "Please let my husband go. We have a child." Her plea brought harsh laughter.

Soon the last line of slaves boarded the ship. As they embarked, her husband cried out, "If we don't meet again in this lifetime, surely we will meet in another."

So the ECKist from Ghana realized it

wasn't mere chance to have met this white German student and develop such a strong attraction for him. It was a past-life connection. She also began to notice an oddity. Whenever he was with her, he behaved like an African. He walked, talked, and gestured like an African.

She used to observe him and wonder, *Now where did he pick that up?*

When this inner experience had ended, the MAHANTA said to her, "Your friend in this lifetime was indeed your husband then."

Finally, she understood the strong rapport between them.

After this she could better handle the faultfinding of her friends, who tried to intimidate her by saying, "You shouldn't be seen with that white man. What will people think?"

This criticism was the voice of the social consciousness speaking. It's an element of the human state that tries to put everybody within a society at the same level. It abhors a taller head in the crowd and attempts to pound all heads to the same social, financial, or philosophical level. This social consciousness is the great leveler. Its spiritual harm comes in its frantic zeal to stamp out individuality.

After this inner experience she drew a firm line with her friends, because now she knew the origin of her affinity for the white German. He was a dear friend from the past. And there she took a stand.

TRAVEL BENEFITS

As you travel to new places, dreams may reveal some past lives you spent there. Such dreams shed light on habits, likes, or fears. They show things gained or lost ages ago. Travel is thus a chance to revisit the foundation of what helped make you who and what you are today.

So take a trip and be aware.

Past-Life Lessons

During my first years in ECK, I had the good fortune to experience many past-life recalls. Some were pleasant. There were also a number of unpleasant ones, recalls of lost opportunities in reaching some desired goal. Not memories to celebrate in the least.

Yet each lifetime, even a supposed failure, gives a fuller understanding about your spiritual nature. You learn about yourself as a spiritual being.

Soul is immortal. It has no beginning or end. It (you) exists because of God's love for It, which is the whole philosophy of ECKANKAR in a nutshell. Our mistakes in this and past lifetimes are the polishings of a precious gem in the rough.

The definition in ECKANKAR of Soul as an immortal being is a valid one. Soul, created in the timeless worlds, existed before birth and endures beyond time and space. God made Soul before the worlds of time and space began. Soul comes to earth from the higher spiritual worlds to add to Its experiences. It inherits many lifetimes for the chance to learn.

And learn It must.

* * *

The next three stories are also from Earth to God, Come In Please . . . , *books 1 and 2. Listen to Dennis Calhoun, Debbie Kaplan, and Beverly Foster tell how the subtleties of karma played out for them.*

God, Who Should I Marry?

By Dennis Calhoun

In college I met a woman, a sure marriage partner. From the first moment it seemed we had always been together, but after graduation, she found a job in Chicago. I landed in Houston. So we kept up a long-distance relationship.

One day during a spiritual exercise I told the Inner Master, the MAHANTA, of my desire to marry.

I explained the need for companionship. If the ECK (Divine Spirit) could work it out, and if it were for the good of everyone, well, that would suit me fine.

Months passed with no resolution to our situation. So we decided to date other people, because it didn't seem likely that I could transfer to Chicago or she to Houston. Soon after, I met a woman, Jaye, and we began to date.

Four months later my company made a big announcement. It would open an office in Chicago, and the plans called for my transfer there. *Perfect!* I thought. I had let go of concern with the situation, and the ECK had opened a way for me to move to Chicago and marry my college sweetheart. But before I left Houston, Jaye shared her feelings with me. She believed we belonged together. She was certain I felt something for her too—and I did.

But in my mind, in my thoughts, I was headed for my girlfriend in Chicago.

After arriving in that city, I soon became engaged. Our relationship was peaceful and calm, as if we had been married before. But then, things began to fall apart. Somehow, our plans to marry no longer felt right to either of us, so with heavy hearts we broke off the engagement.

Once again I took the matter into contemplation. The answer was clear: follow your heart. Go see Jaye.

So far, I had followed my head, and that hadn't worked out. So I called Jaye back in the Houston area. A wonderful feeling rushed into my heart, and I knew I wanted to marry her. But I still didn't understand the reason.

Wasn't it too big of a decision to make purely on the feeling in my heart?

Jaye and I took a trip to New Orleans about a month before the date set for our wedding. While on a walk, we discussed some wedding details. In the French Quarter we turned a corner. Dumbstruck, I stared into a breathtaking courtyard.

That one moment showed me an entire past-life experience.

I turned to Jaye in astonishment and saw that something had happened to her too. We began to talk. Imagine our surprise to discover we'd both had the same vision of a shared past life!

During that incarnation in the late 1850s, I had been a young man in the southern United States. In about 1859, I moved north to find a job to pay for medical school. There I met a northern woman (my college sweetheart in this life). We married. Her parents were wealthy and put me through medical school. Soon after, the Civil War broke out. I returned to the South to serve as a doctor for the Confederacy.

While stationed in New Orleans I met a woman (Jaye, in this lifetime), and we fell in love. But I was married, so we did not act on our love.

Then the war came to an end.

I left New Orleans and returned to my wife in the North. Jaye and I never saw one another again, and I spent the rest of that life living comfortably with the woman I almost married in this life.

After the brief glimpse of this past life, I understood why my relationship with my college girlfriend had been so easy. We had been married before. It also explained why I thought we should marry again. The mind likes familiar and comfortable paths. Still, my heart needed fresh experiences and growth in this life, so it wanted to move on and fulfill the love left behind in New Orleans in that life. Jaye and I have been very happy in our marriage.

Now if I hear two voices—one from my head and one from my heart—I know which is guidance from Divine Spirit. The heart is more often aligned with Soul, the true self.

Thoughts are from the mind. The mind is a good servant, but a poor master.

Now I always tell my friends, "When in doubt, follow your heart!"

A Deadly Race against Time

By Debbie Kaplan

A few months before attending an ECKANKAR seminar, I had a disturbing dream. In the dream I was at the seminar, running to the main auditorium. I opened the doors and looked inside— and every single person in the auditorium was in a wheelchair!

Upon awakening, I couldn't figure out the dream, but I recorded it in my dream journal.

Life went on. About two months later my husband offered to buy me a very nice weight-lifting machine. I accepted his offer, and two men came to my home to set up the machine. It turned out that the proper handlebar for the machine was missing. The installers gave me a bar from an older machine. "It'll be OK," they said. "Use the old bar, and as soon as the new one comes in

42

at the shop, we'll send it out to you."

They left, and I started to try out the machine. Within the first five minutes the handlebar slipped from the machine. My foot was almost severed from my leg.

For one long moment, time stood still.

I stared at my leg. Then I saw the MAHANTA standing next to me. Without words, he told me it was OK. This "accident" was a result of karma from another life. I would be all right.

Things happened fast after that. The ambulance I called whizzed me to the hospital. As the surgeons reconstructed my foot, they told me I was lucky to have survived. But, as Soul, my attention was on the deeper reason for this event. I had to know why. What karmic tie had brought about this horrible accident? I asked the Inner Master to show me a fuller picture of the true cause-and-effect relationship at work in my life.

I discussed some of my dreams, which held the clues to my injury, with a Higher Initiate in ECKANKAR. As he listened the picture became clear.

The karma that caused my injury was with the two men who had delivered and set up the machine. Two lifetimes ago I had caused them similar misfortune which led to their deaths.

I, as Soul, had chosen this lifetime to repay the debt for that transgression against the spiritual laws of life. As I looked further at the past-life records, it was clear that the accident was meant to end this lifetime.

But the MAHANTA had interceded on my behalf.

On the path of ECKANKAR one can work off tremendous amounts of karma in the dream state and through the daily Spiritual Exercises of ECK. Unwittingly, I had been in a race against time. Yet through the grace of the MAHANTA, the Inner Master, enough of the karmic load was lifted so the accident wouldn't cost my life.

Looking back, I realize that I had had a burning desire to study ECKANKAR for three or four years before becoming a student. Now I know why. It was a race against an internal clock. It would have been hard for my five small children if I'd left this life so soon. Now I'll get to see them grow up.

It was also a relief to understand my wheelchair dream—that's my mode of transportation these days. However, I'm very hopeful of one day walking again.

I'm forever grateful to the MAHANTA for the protection and help necessary for me to stay in this life for more spiritual lessons, love, and growth.

Getting Off
Spiritual Welfare

By Beverly Foster

It looked like I had finally used up all my miracles. My husband and I had always lived on the borderline financially. If we had money, we spent like kings. If we didn't, we lived like paupers.

In between, we did our best to control our finances, but we couldn't seem to figure out a way. During those years we leaned on the Holy Spirit. Sure enough, each time we were headed for disaster a miracle intervened.

One year I quit a well-paying job. We hadn't planned how to make our house payments, but my retirement savings and gifts from my family added the needed amount to my husband's income. A few years later my husband started his own computer business. One project was to develop a piece of software. At the same time I changed careers to freelance writing.

From then on whenever we faced certain financial ruin I would sell an article or someone would call from out of the blue to order a computer program. Bonuses at work, unexpected inheritances, gifts when most needed—the evidence mounted to prove that God was taking care of our every need.

One summer we were perched about as far out as possible on the usual cliff. This time, though, the miracles were slow in coming.

I'd quit my job, and now we faced another financial crunch. With luck, if I found a way to make some extra money, and if we could control our spending a little more, we might survive. If not, there was a good chance we'd miss the next house payment.

I awaited a sign from the Holy Spirit that all the good ifs would become reality when I went to the Sunday service at the Temple of ECK. Sri Harold Klemp was the speaker. Excited, I closed my eyes and opened my heart to him.

"Are we going to be better off now?" I asked inwardly.

He'd know what I meant.

Then I sat back for confirmation of my hopes. Instead, three words in his talk went straight to my heart.

"Tighten your belt."

47

While Sri Harold (the Outer Master) spoke this from the stage, the MAHANTA (the Inner Master side of him) added in a loud voice to my inner ear, "This means you!"

Certainly the sign I'd been waiting for, but not what I wanted to hear.

I headed straight for my office after the service to look over our finances. Grimly I asked myself where to cut spending. We had almost stopped buying new clothing. We never went to movies. We only ate out in restaurants once in a while. I shopped at the cheapest grocery store. What else could we do?

As it turned out there was plenty. I added up every paycheck for the next six months, subtracted the bills, then divided the balance by the number of weeks. That was the amount we could spend. No more. The only way to meet our bills was to stick to this plan. At the end of five months we'd be caught up. There'd be extra money for Christmas.

For the first time in our marriage, we had a budget.

Actually, the figures in the budget were quite generous. My husband's income was more than adequate for our needs, but living within it would be hard. And we got no breaks. The kids continued to wear out shoes at a horrendous rate. Nor did we lose our appetites for those occasional pricey restaurant meals. But this time no surprise checks or lucrative job offers came to soften the blow. Still, we managed to stick to the budget—no matter how tight it seemed—for all five months.

At the end of that time it occurred to me to ask the Inner Master what I had done to create this lifetime of financial problems. The answer came gradually through my dreams and contemplations.

One morning before my spiritual exercise I asked the question again: What had I done to create this lifetime of financial problems?

I closed my eyes and sang *HU*, a love song to God. Opening my eyes to my inner vision, I saw a beautiful young woman before me. Her blond hair was cut short in the bobbed style of the day. Green eyes were smudged with dark eyeliner.

In a gentle, almost childish voice she spoke of the corrupting influence of money.

"Look at my father," she said. "He used his money for power and didn't care who got hurt in the bargain."

I could imagine the cruel and capricious parent who had oppressed this woman beyond her limits. To escape, she had run away to finish that lifetime in the gutters of Paris.

When I realized this woman was me in a past life, I could go back and forth between her world and mine, seeing the truth from both points of view. While I had enjoyed the benefits of great wealth in my youth in that lifetime, I had not appreciated them. Wealth was like air, or water, or my own beauty. It was always there. When I did allow myself to think about it, it was with feelings of guilt for having so much while others had so little.

In my contemplation I could see the many opportunities for wealth squandered in this lifetime. The many times I had relied on others to care for me. Relinquishing control over money had absolved me of responsibility and guilt.

So I spoke to the woman, showing her how her attitudes had traveled through time to restrict me in this lifetime. She was in full agreement.

Then she pointed out how my fear of poverty could in the same way prevent me from having valuable experiences in a later incarnation. Surprised, I had to admit she was right. Poverty taught sacrifice and discipline, while abundance brought lessons in discrimination and giving with love. Together we had eliminated these extremes. But in so doing we had thereby wedged ourselves into a very narrow corridor of few new experiences.

We vowed to remove all restrictions.

I came out of contemplation with a great sense of relief.

The cushion in our budget is a little softer now, but things have not changed all that much. We still need to watch our spending. After years with our hands out to Divine Spirit, it's not been easy. But each step toward financial independence brings a greater pride in our own abilities.

So at a time I despaired of miracles, I received the greatest one of all—proof that the MAHANTA's love could teach me to stand on my own two feet.

3
Remembering
Past Lives

*W*hy remember past lives?

We need to understand that the challenges we face today involve all sorts of past-life experiences. Once we gain awareness of these links to other lives, it's possible to handle our challenges in a better way this time around. We can end a chain of karma that has hung on for centuries.

All debts must be repaid before one gains spiritual freedom.

A man in Africa was grieved to learn that his young daughter had died without warning. The mother had taken the child to the hospital for a minor illness, but the head nurse had administered the wrong inoculation. So their daughter passed over to the other side.

The father was distraught. He demanded that the owner of the hospital and the head nurse explain the reason for his daughter's death.

"What have you done?"

"We didn't do anything wrong," they said. "The medicine didn't work."

Yet the answer rang false. In a disturbed state of mind, he found it hard not to strike the nurse in anger and frustration.

The day of the funeral arrived. All the neighbors in the community came to offer condolences. The link between families was a very strong one in that community, and the people had come to help bury the dead child.

As the parents mourned at graveside, a beautiful golden butterfly hovered over the crowd. Then it flew away. As the father looked closer at the dirt around the grave, he spotted a caterpillar. He realized that Soul going into a higher state is like a caterpillar transforming into a butterfly. During the time this butterfly had attended the melancholy gathering, the father also noticed a flock of white-and-blue birds—about a dozen—flying in a circle over the crowd.

In spite of these two spiritual signs of a higher purpose to all this, he remained distraught. He went home and wrapped himself in a sheet. Then he began to sob.

In his grief, he cried, "MAHANTA, why did you allow my daughter to leave like this?"

Soon thereafter he fell into an exhausted sleep. While asleep, he met the MAHANTA, who came to him and said, "Have you learned nothing from the ECK teachings? My son, I have tried to teach you, and yet you carry on like a child."

The scene changed.

In a room that appeared stood his daughter. She ran up and hugged him. After they had hugged awhile, she began to squirm, wanting to get down, run off, and play.

Then the MAHANTA spoke again. "Just wait a minute. Let me show you something. Please hold your daughter."

Like magic, a TV appeared on the wall, and a movie began to play.

The MAHANTA said, "We are now going back to the Oracle at Delphi."

As they watched, a scene formed on the TV screen showing five warriors locked in mortal combat. Two of the warriors were the parents of this girl. His daughter was also in the fray. The scene revealed her as a very strong enemy warrior in that lifetime, and she overpowered two of her parents' tribe. But two warriors—now husband and wife —overcame this powerful warrior (their daughter).

The MAHANTA explained the scene.

"In that lifetime," he said, "your daughter was the very strong warrior who killed these other two in battle. One of the warriors is the owner of the hospital. The other is the head nurse. If you had struck the nurse in the hospital, she would have died, and this would have extended the karma for another round."

"The only way to resolve this karma," the MAHANTA added, "was for your daughter to pay it back here. That would release her from her last life on this earth."

Then the father realized that this collection of characters—himself, wife, daughter, the owner of the hospital, and the head nurse—were not casual strangers. They had been together in that earlier life. The scale of karma was thrown out of balance then. Yet this experience had broken the old karmic chain. It allowed the girl to move ahead in her spiritual life and never have to return to earth. She was now full of light and joy.

As to the reason for her appearance as a warrior in this past-life replay, the MAHANTA said, "That is how you knew her."

Now she had the freedom to go on to a higher and happier place.

Once he saw and understood that, the man awoke and told his wife the dream. They could still grieve the loss of their child, yet it was now possible to understand the reason for this apparent injustice. They realized that her death was justice after all. True justice.

Then they found peace.

Learning about Ourselves

Some years ago on my first visit to Paris, I roamed this fabled city where Roman conquerors had set up a colony at a busy crossroads in 52 BC. It became the capital city of the Franks in the sixth century. In the eighteenth century it lay at the center of the French Revolution. Then, in World War II, captive of the Nazis. Paris today remains the glamorous belle of Europe.

In the airport a woman in her sixties shared a remembrance with considerable pride. No doubt drawing on rich memories from the Second World War, she said, "No single man is safe in Paris. I ought to know—this is my town!"

She'd not been a nun.

Paris had been my town, too, on more than one occasion in recent incarnations.

The last major lifetime there was during Napoleon's ill-fated march on Moscow in 1812.

Napoleon had marshaled half a million troops and crossed the Russian border in June, but by October the Russians had forced his retreat in the biting cold of winter. Only about fifty thousand French soldiers escaped the Russian pursuers. The rest were lost.

Along with other young men of France, I had been compelled to leave wife and home for war. There was no choice in the matter. All able-bodied men received orders to join Napoleon's vast military forces.

The march into Russia began in the summertime, but we saw little of the enemy— except for the major battle at Borodino in September. It was a phantom force that liked to slip away before a major face-to-face encounter.

All through history, the Russian winters have proved a stout ally to the Russian people. Hitler, the reincarnation of Napoleon, tested his luck again in World War II, with the same disastrous results. His armies suffered a rout as convincing as did those of Napoleon in the earlier campaign.

In late autumn, I fell to a grave illness outside Moscow during the ragged retreat of the French army. Here my last days in that lifetime were attended to by a young Russian woman whose family tried folk remedies to restore me from a bout with pneumonia. In this life she is my daughter. All attempts at recovery, though, failed as frostbite ate at what little health remained.

Napoleon had underestimated the enormity of supplying his large army with food and clothing.

As a consequence I left that life a disillusioned man. His shortsighted plans were at the root of our bad luck. They caused my untimely passing. Our summer uniforms, in tatters after the harsh summer campaign, were a thin joke to the Russian bear of winter.

I brought two strong feelings into this life from that period in the early nineteenth century. One is a distaste for cold weather.

The other, a respect for leaders who draw up careful plans before launching big projects.

Character Building

Many people do not know the fact of Soul's rebirth into a succession of lives on earth. Few learn to recall past-life memories so that lessons of long ago can be recaptured for advantage today.

Most run their lives as if this stay were a one-shot deal—the beginning and end of all that's worthy of reflection. Yet is it a crime to say that Soul inhabits a physical body but one time? Or that It never chafed under a master's discipline in a past life? Or that It never took on other incarnations at the death of those bodies, to see rebirth today and advance Its spiritual education?

No, it's not a crime to be ignorant of divine law. Experience is a hard-nosed teacher; time, the great educator.

Our character is made up of virtues and shortcomings, and all are a development from past lives. A reason lurks in the background of every twist of personality. Each trauma from a forgotten life shapes our conduct in a given way. Without exception.

Unless, of course, the force of Divine Spirit enters our consciousness to override the mind's knee-jerk reaction to life's challenges.

Divine law is the beginning and end of all truth. That law includes karma and reincarnation.

KNOWING

When an unexpected situation comes up, you might be surprised you know what to do. In dealing with it, you enjoy a sense of knowing the right steps to take.

Where does this knowing come from?

In a past life, you may have ministered to others as a medic on the battlefield. At some level you carry those memories with you. So when a sudden emergency arises and by second nature you sense the right thing to do, you may be drawing on experiences from the past.

Beginning to Recall

A woman in New York City we'll call Amber has had a fear of icebergs since childhood. To travel from one area of her city to another means a ride on a ferry, and she dislikes boat rides. Nor does she care to swim near rocks. On one vacation in Puerto Rico, the tide had swept her out to some rocks, where she went into a panic and came near drowning.

She'd often wondered about this fear of rocks in water, and her intense fear of boats.

The fear grew in strength as Amber reached adulthood. By then she noticed an absolute terror when seeing even a picture of icebergs.

What would cause such a response?

At one of her ECKANKAR classes, the

group tried a spiritual exercise to view the past. As they did the exercise, she wondered, *Is it possible that I was on the* Titanic *when it sank in 1912?*

Amber went into contemplation to find out. She did begin to see into the past. Yet before allowing an outcome, she cut off the experience and sat waiting for the others to finish the spiritual exercise.

The next night at bedtime she did her usual contemplation. The MAHANTA came and asked, "Why did you cut off the contemplation yesterday?"

"I just felt uncomfortable, and I didn't want to see any more," she replied.

"It's important for you to see and know what's happened in the past," the MAHANTA said, "so that you can live this life without fear."

Titanic Memory

So Amber went into contemplation a second time that evening. The MAHANTA, the Inner Master, let her see the past like a movie, as if she had become an actress in this movie. She was indeed booked as a passenger on the *Titanic*.

But she didn't die on the ill-fated maiden voyage of this famous ship. She was a survivor. One of the women to secure a seat in a lifeboat, she was thus able to save her life. Some men in the water wanted to climb into the lifeboat, but she fended them off. She feared it would sink and threaten her own life.

In this lifetime Amber gave birth to two healthy children, but after these full-term pregnancies she had four boys in a row who died soon after birth. Each lived just a few hours to a few days. Then they died.

What was the reason for this string of heartaches?

In this contemplation scene, Amber saw that her refusal to let the drowning men into the lifeboat was a most selfish act. It denied others the right to live.

That was the reason for her loss of four sons.

A second realization was that in the previous life she'd been born into a selfish family, a family that scorned generosity. And she proved to be the most selfish of them all.

With that understanding of her past, Amber could choose a new direction in this lifetime, one of love and service to others.

Our Karma at Birth

When fear is a dominant player in your life, it steals the joy and freedom of living.

Hidden fears—stacks and stacks, piles and piles of them—reside in each human being. What is their origin? Many fears developed before your birth into this lifetime. Each human being carries a history of hundreds or thousands of past lives. That allows plenty of time to hurt others. And it also gives them a chance to hurt you. Get hurt enough in a certain way, and you cringe from the mere thought of that sort of pain.

People are not born equal. At birth each brings a unique load of karma.

But most people have no idea how to work it off. How many even know it exists? And so they cower inside their coats of flesh, too afraid to live and too scared to die. They desire heaven; earth is hell. Yet they fear the passage to heaven, because the passageway is death.

It's the mother of ironies.

Spiritual Opportunity

Maybe your life has been anything but easy. For all of us life dishes up hard knocks, because they get the job done. It's the best way to learn our spiritual ABCs. The expansion of consciousness finds fertile soil in hardships.

Like you perhaps, I had my share of troubles while growing up. They continue today. Life will crush you, unless you rise above them.

We do whatever it takes to keep strong, to retain our health. We employ our God-given talent of creativity and the ability to listen in order to flourish in every area of life. We do all within our power to thrive. This incarnation is a gold mine, a rich life, worth every ounce of trouble that rebirth brings. And should we abuse the trusts and responsibilities in our care, we learn of better ways in the hot furnace of karmic burn-off. The heat of life teaches us that some things don't make it. In the end, the only thing that counts is love divine.

We come to a conclusion. It's not knowledge, we realize, but a *knowingness* of divine love that holds the key to wisdom and spiritual freedom.

Subconscious Memories

Angry people often spoil for fights of tongue or fist and thus risk a shortened life. The next time around, their conscious memory of past lives is a clean board. Otherwise they'd return with an eye toward gathering sticks, stones, and knives, all the quicker to assail old foes with a vengeance.

That said, however, the subconscious memory of past events does remain.

It is the intuitive memory of past-life deeds of wrong or right. You carry this memory, as we all do to one degree or another.

The subconscious memory of past rights and wrongs done to us explains the reason you may walk into a new job and feel good, right at home. The people seem like old acquaintances. In fact, they are. You knew them in happy circumstances before. Again, the subconscious memory may cut the other way. You could land in a place where someone takes delight in slipping burrs under your saddle. For no known reason. You and Joe Gruff start off on the wrong foot, because you sense he's behind a plot to unseat you and send you out the door.

And you could be right.

Around the Wheel

The subconscious memories of past experiences with associates are but a small portion of the human family's grand circle of karma.

Within the larger circle of human karma, which includes all people of all nations, myriad smaller circles exist. These include still lesser groups. All in all, we find the people of the individual nations, states or provinces, cities, towns, and neighborhoods in the ring of human karma.

In the smaller and most important circles of karma are the intimate realms of friends and families.

In Wisconsin, my birthplace, one was bound to bump into a second or third cousin everywhere within thirty miles of home. Everybody knew everybody. The broad family is a strong karmic group. Yet family circles of karma also cross national borders, into the domains of other governments, where foreign laws set a different tone of interaction upon relatives there. These larger circles of Souls all rest upon the immediate, the nuclear, family. And within this tight group—husband, wife, and children—opposing states of thought and action pose a day-to-day challenge.

Why the strife? A family is an intimate group that learns spiritual grace by its members bumping into each other, thereby smoothing over rough edges.

Various scenarios play out within each family circle. In one case, a boy may suffer mistreatment by his father. So when the boy grows up, he mistreats his own children. Time sees him grow old, weak, and helpless. Then an adult offspring, who has the care of him, may relish the opportunity to return the favor and neglect the old man's needs.

And so enmity takes an ever firmer grip and perpetuates itself into another generation.

Still, all meet again in the future to face each other, in mixed roles, eager to continue the ages-long karmic battle. So father may return as girl, mother as father, boy as mother, plus the happy mishmash of some uncles, aunts, and cousins tossed into this karmic salad.

That's the way of karma.

Friedrich von Longau, in *Retribution*, caught the spirit of karmic action in the human arena. He writes, "Though the mills of God grind slowly / Yet they grind exceeding small."

There is no way off this wheel of reincarnation until each person learns about the Light and Sound of God. They lift the individual above the petty self, above human nature.

* * *

The following story is from Earth to God, Come In Please . . . , *book 1. Mr. Spaulding shows how the MAHANTA helped him resolve a sticky karmic situation with his employer. Things turned much worse before they got better.*

A Business Challenge
By Ed Spaulding

My job was going well. I was a salesman for a printing company and had landed a number of large accounts. My commissions were increasing every month, and I was happy and excited about the future.

One day the owner of the company, Dave, called me into his office. "Ed," he said, "I want you to sign a new contract." It retroactively lowered commissions which he had yet to pay me. I would lose over ten thousand dollars. The new contract also put a limit on my future earnings.

When I voiced a protest, Dave said, "You're making more than your job is worth. I have to restructure your commissions."

In shock at the sudden turn of events, I muttered something about needing time to look over the contract, then stumbled from his office.

I put off signing the contract for several days. The more I tried to negotiate with Dave, the angrier and more intimidating he became. When I sat down to do my spiritual exercises, I realized I was caught in a web of emotional and mental turmoil. Trying to talk with Dave was draining me. I was hurt by his unwillingness to communicate. At last, he gave an ultimatum: "Sign the contract, or you're fired!"

I realized I didn't trust him anymore. How could I then keep working for him?

Within myself I began to sing *HU*, the love song to God, to keep in balance. I said, "Dave, I quit. But I want to be paid what is owed me according to the old commission structure."

Dave flew into a rage. His face turned as red as a beet. He shoved me out of the building, and I felt lucky to escape without injury.

As I drove away I felt relief. But he'd cheated me out of a lot of money. So terrified was I of Dave that I didn't know whether it was worth the trouble to go after my lost commissions.

Partly out of avoidance and partly because of needing a break from the tension, I stopped thinking about the situation. I calmed down and soon began a new business in another area of the printing field.

One day, while driving to my new office, I noticed a large rusty car trailing me. Waves of fear and anger washed over me. Dave was having me followed. A game of cat and mouse ensued as I let the other car pass and then tried to catch up with it, but it escaped in traffic.

Later, looking out my office window, I saw the same rusty heap at a stop sign. My heart began to pound. I chanted *HU* to myself, asked for divine protection, and ran out to confront the driver. Questioning my own sanity I knocked on the window of the rusty car.

The man swore at being caught. He rolled down the window and shouted, "I should be beating you up right now."

In my most calming voice, I said, "Why is Dave paying you to follow me?"

"Dave says you're out to destroy his business. He told me you needed to be watched. He even offered me a two-hundred-dollar bonus if I would beat you up!"

I stared in openmouthed amazement. He continued, "My brother said you were a nice guy. He knows you from work and advised me not to do it." As the man drove off, I stood wondering, *Why was my life suddenly transformed into a bad TV movie?*

There was no avoiding Dave now. My anger was stronger than my fear. I called and said, "You better stop having me followed!"

He denied everything and instead accused me of stealing his customers. If I didn't stop, he would sue me. Hanging up the phone, I realized it was time to see a lawyer. I needed to know my rights. Picking a law office out of the phone book, I made an appointment.

The night before going to see the lawyer, I had a vivid dream of being back in Dave's office. His wife came up to me, her face filled with fear and desperation. "Please, Ed," she said, "don't you and the lawyer put us through this again."

She even mentioned a lawyer's name.

Then Dave came up. "I'm going to sue you!" he said.

To my surprise, though, he didn't try to throw me out of the office. Instead he said, "As long as you're here, the least you can do is help out." He was working on a job I'd once sold for him, so I joined in.

To make the job work, I had to fold up the contract he'd wanted me to sign and wedge it under a chart to keep it from slipping.

The dream shifted. Now I was in my home, where the same piece of paper came back from Dave in the mail. On it was written the amount of money that would settle our differences.

Then I awoke. I wrote down the dream and felt encouraged. But it was time to rush off and meet my new lawyer. When I arrived, it was a shock to discover that the attorney on my case had the same name Dave's wife had spoken in the dream!

Showing the lawyer my documents,

I described the situation. His eyes lit up with dollar signs.

"This will be an easy case to win," he said. Perhaps he sensed some reluctance on my part, because he added, "I'll even waive the normal retainer to get us started. Just sign here."

Instead, I just sat there. My thoughts returned to my dream and what it meant.

It seemed that if I sued Dave, it would be a repeat of an old play from a past life. If there were only another way to work things out. Then, our karma would resolve once and for all. So I asked the lawyer for time to think things over and left.

Later, in contemplation, I spoke of my frustration to the MAHANTA. I asked to see the past life that had caused such intense conflict between Dave and me.

The MAHANTA said, "You'll see these past lives in time. For now, I'll arrange a meeting with Dave, Soul to Soul, to begin to work out your karma."

In my contemplation the MAHANTA

opened a door. In walked Dave, smiling and full of light. It was great to see him happy and willing to talk. Here, in a higher state of consciousness, we shared the goal of resolving all karma between us.

So I asked him about the behavior of his human consciousness.

"I'm afraid of you!" he said.

This was amazing, since I was afraid of him. I then asked, "Well, how can we work things out on the outer, since I can't speak with you?"

Dave smiled and said calmly, "A way will be provided."

I thanked him and the MAHANTA, because now I was beginning to feel things could work out.

A few days later I received a very threatening letter from Dave's lawyer. But at the end of the letter it said to call him if I had any questions. "Aha!" I cried. "This is the way Dave has provided for communication."

The meeting with my lawyer had

convinced me I was in a position of legal strength. So I called Dave's lawyer and explained my case to him. I told him all I wanted was the commission owed me. Later in the day Dave's lawyer called back. Although he'd obviously had a rough session with his client, he had convinced Dave to pay me in full!

For the next year, I received monthly checks from him in the mail. This monthly income enabled me to sustain myself while I built my own business, a goal I'd had for some time.

I realized that the experience with Dave had strengthened me. It had given me the courage to take the risk of forming my own business. Next to the risk of enduring a new difficult boss, starting my own venture seemed easy.

After a year, Dave's lawyer called. "Dave's willing to meet with you to reach a final agreement," he informed me.

Preparing to call Dave and set up an appointment, I realized I was still terrified of him. So I went into contemplation and met him again, Soul to Soul.

I asked, "Would you please tell me what you need to keep your composure when we meet?"

When I called Dave, the first thing he said to me was, "We'll sit down and go over the books. But I can't handle any discussion. Please respond to me in writing."

I realized this was what he needed to keep his balance, so I agreed. There were two tense meetings. I kept my promise not to argue with him in person, so we resolved our differences on paper, struck an agreement, and went our separate ways.

Shortly after our last meeting I had a vision. I saw Dave and me in a past life where he had cheated me in a business situation. I had responded in a vindictive manner, ruining his business. In a moment it was clear that Dave's tremendous anger in this life was a mirror of my own hatred from the past. It was coming back to me in the present.

To work off the karma for ruining his old business, I helped Dave build his present company into a success. When he cheated me in this life, it was a golden opportunity for me to grow spiritually. I could work things out in a balanced way, while facing my own anger at myself and him from the past.

In forgiving Dave, I was forgiving myself.

A year and a half later I ran into Dave on the street. To my surprise, instead of getting into his car, he came over. He smiled and shook my hand.

"Just after our last meeting I had a severe heart attack," he said. "I nearly died. The doctor told me I had to sell my business if I wanted to live."

Dave had spent the past year traveling around the world with his family, having a wonderful time. He commented, "It's great to get to be the nice guy in life. My only regret from the business was how I treated you."

Quietly, Dave apologized to me. I accepted his apology with tears in my eyes, and we were both swept with a wave of emotion.

I felt the presence of the MAHANTA. With it came the knowingness that, at long last, our karma was healed.

As I looked into Dave's eyes, I recognized the beautiful Soul I had met on the inner, now outwardly manifested.

4

Death as a Continuum of Life

A woman we'll call Lana kept a female cat for a pet. They'd lived together for eleven years and enjoyed a strong love bond, but in time the cat died. Of course, Lana missed her longtime friend.

About a year after the cat's passing, Lana noted a series of clear dreams.

In one dream, someone said, "Your cat will reincarnate on Monday, July 31." When Lana awoke, she thought, *That dream was nice, but I live in an apartment in a big city now. I don't know how my cat will find me.*

Then came a second dream.

In this dream someone handed her two kittens. Both kittens were striped; one was lighter, the other darker. The MAHANTA, the Inner Master, said, "The darker of the two is yours."

That same week one of her friends called. "Two of my cats had litters at the same time," she said. "Would you like a kitten?"

When Lana went to look at one of the litters, she saw the striped kittens from her dream. "This is my cat," she said, picking up the darker of the two.

"It's a male," said her friend. Lana paused.

"A male?" she said. "My cat was a very feminine female. I can't imagine her coming back as a male cat." She felt a sudden unease about her dream.

But her friend said, "If you want a female, there's a lovely gray-and-white kitten in the other litter. This kitty loves everybody." But it didn't love Lana. "I think I'd better stick with the striped one," Lana said, releasing the clawing bundle of fur.

On her way out Lana asked, "By the way, what was the mother cat's name?"

"Z," came the reply. (Z is another name for the Inner Master, Wah Z.) As she drove home, she thought, *Maybe this really is my cat, even though it's a male.*

Later, for contemplation, she opened an ECK book at random. It read "Soul will alternate between male and female bodies, each time learning some lessons while gathering karma and working off karma."

Lana had her answer. The striped male kitten was her old friend come back.

Fear of Death

The greatest fear of all is the fear of death, say pundits.

They avow that everything about it has already been said. That is true in part. However, the poetic Preacher of Ecclesiastes has an eloquent way of placing death in perspective with the experiences of life. "To everything there is a season," he says, "and a time to every purpose under the heaven:

A time to be born, and a time to die. . . . A time to weep, and a time to laugh; a time to mourn, and a time to dance."

We think we know the meaning of detachment until one of our own passes to the other side. Then we're not sure. We wonder, *Where is God in this our sorrow?*

The philosophers of old grappled with the matter of death too. Epicurus, the Greek philosopher of the third century BC, taught that the physical senses are infallible in determining truth. What a misunderstanding. Yet he did make an interesting point.

"There is nothing terrible in living to a man who rightly comprehends that there is nothing terrible in ceasing to live," he said.

Lucretius, the Roman philosopher and poet, felt that death should be of no concern at all. When Soul leaves the body, he said, It ceases to exist. Life is swallowed up in death.

A hopeless and gloomy philosophy if ever there was one.

But the searing light of truth as taught in ECKANKAR is like a flaming arrow, because it pierces the shell of such grim philosophies. ECKANKAR teaches the freedom of Soul. Soul triumphs over death. It is a spark of God. Its very existence rests upon the divine breath of Holy Spirit, the ECK, the sacred Light and Sound.

Therefore, Soul is the victor; death, the vanquished.

Now consider birth.

Birth is the miracle by which Soul enters a new physical body. It's the opening chapter of our life, while death marks the last. But death's victory is brief. Our first cries as a newborn, like the probing fingers of dawn, herald an awakening from a night of rest.

Soul is eternal. That is Its heritage. Through ageless cycles of the miracle of birth, Soul continues Its quest to become more like Its Creator. It's like a bee that must find the nectar.

An individual matures, then dies; his atoms return to dust. Yet before ages pass, the Lords of Karma stir the dust to create a new body for him. And so he begins another round on the wheel of life.

Death is thus a passing from one chapter of life to another, and from there to still another. The process is a natural one. It's been a part of your experience many times in the past. But you can stop this cycle. The teachings of ECK show how you, too, can find spiritual freedom in this very lifetime.

Seeing Death from Above

An acquaintance told of an out-of-body experience he'd had in his early forties. For the sake of privacy, we'll call him Andy. A heart attack struck him down. Then an ambulance rushed him to the hospital where doctors did everything in their power to save his life.

In the middle of all the confusion, Andy had left his body. Hovering near the ceiling like a pair of eyes, he felt a great happiness. There was no concern about the fate of his pale physical body stretched out below on the operating table. Then a doctor injected a potent drug. A powerful force drew him back to his unconscious body, though he had no desire to return to it.

Later, Andy told a nurse of this out-of-body adventure in the operating room while his body lay unconscious. But none of the staff put much stock in his story.

At last, he decided to keep the experience to himself. The medical staff was giving him odd looks, because they feared his mind had suffered damage from a lack of oxygen.

* * *

Another ECKist recalled a similar story about his dad, whom we'll call Carl. Carl told his children about the time a serious illness had brought him to a hospital in critical condition. Carl told this story so that his children would not go through life with a fear of death.

Here's what Carl told them.

His heart had stopped beating. A doctor had no luck in trying to start it. All this happened years ago, before medical knowledge had advanced to its present state. The family vet happened to be present. He hammered both fists on the stricken father's chest, trying to restart the failed heartbeat.

Carl, in the meantime, went outside his body. From a point near the ceiling, he enjoyed a commanding view of the whole scene. He watched the frantic attempts of the two doctors below.

Then his attention switched to a new scene. He found himself climbing a spiral staircase. An enchanting melody beckoned him on, ever higher up the stairs. There was no desire to return to his body. Then he faced a doorway, sensing that if he passed through it, his earthly life would end. So he started for the door. It seemed like a gift from heaven.

In desperation, at that exact moment, the veterinarian dealt his chest the sharpest blows yet. This enraged Carl. The extreme pounding was drawing him away from the doorway that promised a life of eternal peace. He awoke, railing and cursing. The doctors and nurses supposed the outburst to be a case of delirium and so ignored him. Patients did that sort of thing.

After this Soul experience, Carl lost all fear of death.

What an upbeat story to pass along to one's children.

But let's return to the hospital now for later evidence of Carl's out-of-body experience.

One of the doctors had lost his pen during the excitement brought on by Carl's crisis. When Carl confided to a nurse what had occurred while his body lingered near death, she dismissed his tale. Imagine her shock when he told her where to locate the doctor's pen. None dared believe his story. However, they were hard put to explain how he knew the location of the lost pen, which had eluded the medical staff's best attempts to find it.

Carl is not a student of ECKANKAR. But his son, who told the story, has been a student for some years.

"My dad isn't an ECKist," he said, "but as far as he's concerned, ECKANKAR makes more sense than a lot of that other stuff."

Take it from one who knows.

* * *

Both of the above men, each having had an experience of being outside the body, are strong individuals. Fears of sin or guilt don't trouble them. They take responsibility for their thoughts and actions. Nor do they bend to pressure to become a member of one religion or another. They know their own minds.

A disguised threat like "Join us or risk damnation" is fire without heat—of no effect at all.

In early American lingo, these two are salts. They have crossed the creek and scaled the mountain.

A large number of people in the United States claim at least one vision. This category may include a strong, unforgettable dream or an out-of-body experience.

Whatever form the experience takes, it is a wake-up call from God.

From that time on, many become seekers. Yet they may continue this lifetime in the church of their youth, unwilling to upset a family or social framework by leaving that community of worshippers for ECKANKAR. Many acknowledge, however, that ECKANKAR does offer more real answers to spiritual questions than does their church.

So they are seekers.

Perhaps in the next lifetime, they will muster the courage to embrace truth. They will pose the age-old questions that all seekers ask: "What is my purpose? What is the meaning of life?"

Then the Master appears.

Your Destiny as Soul

Soul enters this world to pursue a series of tasks, for each is an exercise in spiritual purification. Taken as a whole, these assignments make up one's destiny. To set the tone for Its mission, Soul enters a new lifetime with a body of strength, or weakness; into wealth, or poverty; of great intellect, or a simple mind; in a popular shade of skin, or not; either as a male, or a female.

The idea of destiny as a concept is out of fashion in much of today's Western society. People want to be captains of their own lives. They wish to run their own fate. They will shape their own tomorrows. Yet how can they do so without a knowledge of and an appreciation for the meticulous Law of Karma?

Or especially, of the Law of Love?

In spite of all fictions about who is the master of their own fate, they cannot even set the conditions of their birth. And so the rules of karma and reincarnation remain a mystery, and they find a great deal of sorrow and disappointment in the outcome of their plans.

How could the stiff rules of karma include them?

Many would like to think they don't, sure of being above the common pool of humanity and thus exempt from these rules.

By and large, though, the Lord of Karma—not the individual—selects a family for each Soul. Soul must then follow the script of destiny and enter a physical body.

The Lord of Karma is like a minor's guardian. He administers a trust on behalf of a spiritual infant, arranging for him or her to join a family with the best prospect for that Soul's unfoldment. In selecting the time and place of reincarnation, the Lord of Karma is the sole judge. He is the sole arbiter in the choice of a body, health, family, or future. The Lord of Karma alone sets the conditions of most people's fate.

Placement is a simple karmic detail. The Law of Karma governs all such placements, and he is only its agent.

The primal seed for each incarnation exists under the umbrella of destiny, which we also call past-life karma. On a practical level, genetic, cultural, and social elements combine to decide Soul's place in this world. For people on the lower end of the survival scale, the Lord of Karma alone chooses the time and place of rebirth.

After birth, then, the name of the game

is survival. The survival scale, by definition, is a measure of one's can-do instincts.

But karmic placement does set other standards for individuals on the high end of the spiritual scale. More of them enjoy a voice in the choice of a human body or place of birth. They sense the need for spiritual freedom, a view gained from many past lives, and the self-responsibility that goes along with the package. So these Souls demonstrate creative ideas and inventiveness in their incarnations. For the most part they are cheerful, upbeat people.

Spiritual gains in past lives have given them a voice in choosing some of the conditions in their present incarnation.

They have earned the right.

Think of destiny as the equipment, talents, or gifts that one brings to this life. They carry a divine mandate to use them for the good of all life. It's our responsibility to do so, with wisdom.

The idea of destiny, or fate, is poked fun at in many Western circles. Yet it is an age-old principle of the spiritual life.

What is the basis for a cultural bias against fate?

People are in a state of confusion about it. They wonder, *How can fate and free will exist side by side?* Destiny controls the conditions at birth. Much of what an individual does after birth is an open book, an exercise in free will. Free will can offset or even overcome the drawbacks of destiny, but only through the awakening of one's consciousness. One may thus reshape both his material and spiritual life.

To sum up, fate governs the conditions at birth; free will allows a choice as to how to move beyond them.

Lessons from Each Life

A past life was a moving force in teaching you compassion for others, even though in that life you showed no empathy for the suffering of others. At times, perhaps, playing the role of torturer, cruel lord, or even terrorist. A later life, then, to restore balance to the karmic scale, demanded you suffer the indignities of a victim. So you become the tortured, the oppressed, and the violated.

It's all in the game.

Each lifetime teaches at least one lesson and often dozens.

Of course, other lifetimes were routine ones. With no monumental lessons, they nonetheless served as an opportunity for healing and reflection. You may have jockeyed from an early lifetime of adventure to a later one of rest. People do return to earth to heal. They squirrel away in a quiet place in some pastoral setting, a token reminder of the heaven they left behind.

Bless the likes of hermits, shepherds, and homebodies. They have their place.

Learning about Love

A European man told this story about his elderly father and mother.

One day the father, call him Aaron, suffered a stroke, and an ambulance rushed him to the hospital. Recovering in a few weeks, he returned home though still weak.

Soon thereafter came a second shock. Doctors found his wife had a terminal illness and gave her but a few short days. She was comfortable with life yet showed no fear of death. She took the news in stride. She told Aaron not to worry, then entered a hospital. The doctors, who'd been witness to similar crises in other families, were astounded by her serenity.

During the final days of separation, husband and wife missed each other, of course.

Then Aaron's mate tried an experiment. She used an imaginative technique to be with her beloved. Later she explained to her son that she simply imagined herself at home in bed with Aaron. The first night of her experiment, Aaron woke the next morning and told his son an odd thing.

"Your mother was here beside me in bed last night."

The son, an ECKist who understood the ways of Divine Spirit and knew of the love bond between his parents, expressed his happiness for them.

The few precious days passed. The couple often shared their nights in this way, and soon Aaron began to hear a celestial sound of ECK. He confided to his son that he had never heard the songs of birds with such clarity. He could distinguish the birds by their songs.

Yet, in fact, these sounds were not of earthbound birds at all, but from the Holy Spirit, or ECK. The Voice of God was manifesting to him like birdsongs. It was the off-season for such birds.

Aaron's wife translated, or passed on, ten days after she entered the hospital. Before her passing she made a last visit to him in a dream, in some heaven on the inner planes. She said she would not see him for three days; she'd be busy with experiences on a number of inner planes.

But she'd return.

She explained the whole matter in a way he could understand. Dying was like moving to a new state or province, so she'd be collecting such things as a driver's license and vehicle registration, new lodgings, and the like.

On the fourth day after her death, Aaron awoke and spoke to his son.

"I saw your mother last night. She was young and beautiful and dressed in her nurse's uniform the way she'd looked when we met during World War II."

A short time later the son, passing his father's room, noticed his sister by their father's bedside and so entered the room. Aaron opened his eyes.

"It's all right," said the son. "It's only me."

But Aaron looked beyond him. As if seeing someone else enter the room, he opened his eyes wide in amazement. They told of neither fear nor dread, but of joy. At that very moment he slipped from his body in peace, joining his dear one in the green fields of heaven.

The radiant smile on the father's lips

was testimony to love's transcendence over death.

The son felt deep gratitude for the chance to witness his father's passing from his tired and worn body. This occasion marked a turning point in his spiritual life too.

The joyful experience of attending his parents' passing taught him many lessons about the power of love over all things, including death.

A Series of Steps

Life is a series of steps. We lurch from point to point, in one lifetime, then another. Such a period in time may offer excitement, burnout, or any other state—whether it should endure a lifetime or an hour. Then again, pleasant and quiet intervals will grant seasons for reflection and contemplation, to give leisure to glance ahead or back, to take stock of lessons in our schooling.

A period of reflection or contemplation awakens a yearning for truth. It will rouse a more fervent desire for love.

Then the teachings of ECK appear.

Life and death have no real boundaries. Death is but a gateway, yet life encompasses all things. In ECKANKAR, we learn to live, move, and have our being within the grand sea of life's endless rhythm.

On occasion, little beams of warm sunshine illumine the cold, dark moments of our lives. This sunshine is God's love. When we let its warmth into our hearts and minds, it routs darkness and fear. When love has conquered all our fear, we have finished the need for future lives on this planet. We rise to a higher state. We are able to bask in the greater blessings of our Creator.

And so the power of karma and reincarnation is reined in.

More spiritual freedom is ours.

* * *

Dee and Kathie recount true stories about the mysterious link between life and death. These accounts are from Earth to God, Come In Please . . . , *books 1 and 2.*

Pop's Reincarnation

By Dee Meredith

As a student of ECKANKAR I often wondered how to prove reincarnation to myself. Were my flashbacks of previous lives just imagination?

Some time ago, my father translated (died). I didn't attend his burial service but was honored to be present inwardly as he awoke in the Astral world. Before long he was up and about, learning about his new home in the inner worlds.

Every so often I would stop in during my spiritual contemplations to see how he was. It was amusing to find that the spiritual principles we had discussed before his death were becoming a reality for him now.

These inner visits went on for about ten months. But one day when I stopped by to chat with Pop, he wasn't in. At first I thought he'd just gone off to explore and would return. But when I asked the Inner Master, he said Pop was preparing for another incarnation on earth. I was surprised but realized that as Soul, Pop must continue on.

One day at work I heard a soft voice inside telling me to watch for my father's incarnation in a few months. I wondered about this. I couldn't think of any woman I knew who was pregnant.

Then I remembered meeting a young couple just after my dad's translation. We'd become fast friends; I felt I had known them for years. She was pregnant now, and I had a knowingness that Dad would return as her baby.

I went to visit my friend the day she came home from the hospital. Everyone was crowded around the baby when I arrived. Catching my first glimpse of the newborn, I noticed his physical structure was like my dad's former human body. The child had the same unmanageable fine hair and yellowish complexion that ran in our bloodline.

In silence, I welcomed this Soul back as I picked up the baby. With intent alertness, his little untrained eyes made an effort to focus on me. I touched his Third Eye with my forefinger. A golden light radiated outward and engulfed his entire head, as his three-day-old baby face twisted into a lopsided grin of recognition.

He strained to move his vocal cords. With a great effort he screamed out my nickname! His new parents were speechless. A ripple of love spread through the room, and we all began to laugh.

In that moment, a wealth of information passed between the baby and me. It was an instant swapping of information, Soul to Soul. One thing I sensed was that Dad felt scrunched up in that tiny body!

I keep track of this Soul through his parents. When I drop by for a visit every so often and he hears my voice, a familiar, lopsided grin brightens his face in welcome.

A Special Feeling of Love

By Kathie Matwiv

I work as a nurse in a terminal ward. Patients die there every day. As an ECK-ist, I have a golden opportunity to practice divine love and compassion.

The first time I met Mike, I knew a karmic link had brought us to this place. Feeling a strong, unconditional love for him, I wanted to make his last days as comfortable as possible.

One day I was wiping his face as he slipped in and out of consciousness. *What past life*, I wondered, *brought us here?*

Looking at his face while relaxing and thinking of the MAHANTA, I heard the distinct report of single-shot rifles. My Spiritual Eye opened. Then I saw myself as a young soldier being shot in the chest.

Another soldier, whom I recognized as Mike in this life, ran to my side. He lifted me over his shoulder, carried me to a ditch, and spoke to me of God as I died.

Now, in this life, our positions were reversed. The brief vision explained my special feeling of love for him. When he died a few days later I was there, singing *HU* and telling him of the divine Light and Sound and the Inner Master, the MAHANTA. I was even given the opportunity to comfort his mother and brother.

How great the joy to repay a debt of gratitude with true spiritual understanding.

5
Spiritual Exercises to Recall and Resolve Past Lives

$\mathcal{M}$any of our dreams relate to past lives. Once we come to that realization, we can begin to access the experiences that lie hidden within our memory banks. And, yes, it is possible to bring hard-won lessons from past lives into the present for a better understanding of our situation in life today.

What are the means of accessing this wealth of experience?

Begin with one of the easy spiritual exercises given in this chapter.

The key to the knowledge and wisdom gained long ago in the school of hard knocks is inside you. This key is true desire. You must want to make spiritual headway when embarking upon a study of dreams to profit from your past lives.

So what is the heart of this quest to be?

Let it be a true desire to become a better human being.

Love and mercy are the stuff of life. A study of dreams has the power to open your heart to the essence of your real self. Who are you? These spiritual exercises can help you reach out to learn the answer and find the secret to self-mastery.

Read the spiritual exercises that follow. Then choose for practice the one with most appeal to you. Work with it. See where it leads you.

Later, do the same with each of the other exercises.

The Movie Screen Method
(To Find Your Inner Guide)

Find a comfortable position and relax. Shut your eyes. Now look at an inner screen, and imagine you are viewing a movie screen. It may be black, white, or even gray. In time, a lifelike scene or moving picture should appear.

Look right at the screen. After a while, let your inner vision shift a bit to either the left or right of it. From the corner of your eye, look for any movement on the screen.

This is a useful method to search for your inner guide.

In a relaxed manner, then, look off to either side of the mental screen, knowing full well that your attention is, in fact, on its center. Now sing *HU* or some other holy name of God.

Do this spiritual exercise while singing *HU*, for it starts a purifying, cleansing action within you (Soul). Old habit patterns

113

like a lack of confidence, idle chatter, fear, and self-deception will begin to lose their hold on you.

Watch love replace them.

The Sherlock Holmes Technique

If a problem or question troubles you, try the following exercise to see whether its roots are buried in a past life.

First, shut your eyes. Then, in your mind's eye, imagine Sherlock Holmes sporting his funny-looking, double-billed cap. Jump-start your imagination by visualizing a luminous blue shape. Watch it crystallize into the tall, lanky form of Sherlock Holmes with a magnifying glass in hand. He's coming along a path. As the detective draws near, you see that he is, in fact, the MAHANTA, the Living ECK Master.

He greets you, then says, "If you'll come with me, we'll find a solution to your problem."

Take up his offer and accompany him. The incredible blue light about him is like a dazzling shield. You note that the light passing through his magnifying glass acts like a flashlight. Together you enter a misty marsh.

The Blue Light of ECK illuminates the path.

On this walk with the MAHANTA, chant the word *HUUUACH* (HU-akh). It's similar to HU. This word goes with this exercise. Continue to walk with the Inner Master, who, you recall, is dressed like the famous detective.

Soon, an enormous rock blocks the path. The MAHANTA, still dressed as Sherlock, lifts it without effort. He holds his magnifying glass for you to see through. The blue light shining through the glass turns white. There, emblazoned on the bottom of the rock, you see the solution to your problem.

Do this exercise every other night for a month, switching it with your usual spiritual exercise. That will bypass the resistance of the mind.

See what discoveries await in the secret hollows of your being.

The Radio Announcer Technique

Do you feel there are mislaid pieces of information about some aspect of your life—for example, a disturbing dream or a problem—that feels like a link to a past life? If so, try this technique to help fill in the missing pieces.

Go into contemplation. That means shut your eyes but open your heart and mind.

Now listen for the Sound of ECK. It may be any common, familiar sound. Or, there may be silence too.

Visualize turning on a radio. Next, imagine an announcer's voice filling the airwaves. Listen to him sum up the highlights of the dream or problem whose meaning is unclear to you.

Sing *HU* for a few minutes to relax. This

pause is like taking a commercial break.

Then imagine the radio announcer saying, "And now, here's the rest of your dream." Let him fill in the missing pieces of the dream and thus unravel its meaning.

In the case of a bad or frightening dream, you can be sure the dream censor has not allowed the whole story to come out. So begin with the assumption that something is missing. You don't know all the details. Then let your inner faculties get the answer via this Radio Announcer technique.

A solution could come during this spiritual exercise, but it may appear later in a dream. Again, you may awaken with a clear understanding of your dream or problem.

So be aware.

The Formula Technique

Like so many other ECKists who practice contemplation or enjoy dream travel, I'd have adventures on the inner planes. But how to tell where the experience took place?

Was it on the Astral, Causal, or Mental Plane?

Of course, these planes differ in spiritual importance to us. However, when an inner experience did occur in my early years in ECK, I was often at a loss to tell in which spiritual region it took place.

One night the ECK Master Peddar Zaskq gave me a technique to determine one's location in the other worlds. "It's like a visitor's pass to a certain plane," he said. "Anyone can use it, whether a First Initiate or a Fourth. Instead of just letting the experience happen and then hoping for a signpost later, here are four exercises to help you discover your location in the higher worlds."

Then he gave these four exercises of the Formula technique.

The Physical Plane, he said, is the first level of existence. Right above it lies the second, the Astral Plane. The Causal Plane is third in line. The Mental Plane is next.

Formula Two (there is no Formula One)

118

is for explorations on the Astral Plane, the second level. Chant *HU*, the love song to God, two times, then breathe twice without chanting *HU*. Continue this technique for fifteen minutes before bed or in contemplation. All the while, lightly hold in mind your desire to see and explore the Astral (emotional) Plane.

Ask the MAHANTA, the inner guide, to show you an important past-life record from a previous life on the Physical Plane. It may shed light on mood swings, likes and dislikes, and unreasonable fears.

Formula Three is ideal for the third plane, the Causal. Follow the same procedure as for Formula Two, except now chant three times and breathe three times (without chanting *HU*). This plane contains the seed of all karma. Before falling asleep, imagine yourself on the Causal Plane at the Hall of Records. It is a repository of past-life records on the Physical and Astral Planes, the two planes below the Causal.

Formula Four is for the fourth plane, the

Mental. Chant *HU* four times, then breathe in a normal way four times. This plane is the home of math, architecture, philosophy, higher ideas, and arts along this line.

Formula Five is for the Soul Plane: five HUs and five breaths. The Fifth Plane is the dividing line between the lower, material planes and the higher ones of pure Spirit. It is also the place of our Soul records, a detailed account of our past lives on all the lower planes—the Physical, Astral, Causal, and Mental regions.

Before you begin an exercise, write in your dream journal which exercise of the Formula technique you will try. After you gain a degree of success with an exercise, begin to compare all experiences from the same plane. See the common thread woven through each of them. Note the unique texture of experiences on the Astral level in comparison to the Causal Plane when trying to view past lives.

This technique is a very good one. Try it tonight.

Downloading-the-File Technique

Past-life information from the dream state may appear like a digitized computer file. The ECK Masters can impart knowledge to you by a highly compact form of communication, much like telepathy.

Now imagine downloading the Master's inner discourse to your computer or device. The program or app will do its best to honor the intent of the discourse as it converts the telepathic-like communication into everyday text or speech. However, no computer program can render an exact translation of an inner communication.

So catch the spirit of the message.

By all means, don't worry if your dreams don't play out as described here. The mere practice of this spiritual exercise has power. It releases the latent, invisible force that will convey a necessary past-life recall to you in some way or other.

This method is, at heart, a means to trigger past-life recall.

An Easy Way to Resolve Karma

If you feel the burden of past-life karma in your life, here's an easy way to resolve a good part of it.

Do all deeds in the name of God or the MAHANTA, the Living ECK Master. Let each task hold all your love. Even a humble chore like sweeping the kitchen floor deserves the full span of your love for the Divine Being.

This technique brings love to the fore. An activity performed with divine love burns off karma and affords a spiritual blessing. Often, someone with a creative mind can modify this exercise and develop it as a way to Soul Travel. Listen to the Inner Master. If you have the spiritual preparation, Soul Travel allows more flexibility when exploring the higher worlds.

Do this exercise every day for a week or so. You will find life teaching you subtle ways in which to listen to the MAHANTA, the Living ECK Master speak via the inner channels.

GiftofHU.org

Scan to learn more about HU.

About the Author

Award-winning author, teacher, and spiritual guide Sri Harold Klemp helps seekers reach their full potential.

He is the MAHANTA, the Living ECK Master and spiritual leader of ECKANKAR, the Path of Spiritual Freedom. He is the latest in a long line of spiritual Adepts who have served throughout history in every culture of the world.

Sri Harold teaches creative spiritual practices that enable anyone to achieve life mastery and gain inner peace and contentment. His messages are relevant to today's spiritual needs and resonate with every generation.

Sri Harold's body of work includes more than one hundred books, which have been translated into eighteen languages and won multiple awards. The miraculous, true-life stories he shares lift the veil between heaven and earth.

In his groundbreaking memoir, *Autobiography of a Modern Prophet*, he reveals secrets to spiritual success gleaned from his personal journey into the heart of God.

Find your own path to true happiness, wisdom, and love in Sri Harold Klemp's inspired writings.

Next Steps in Spiritual Exploration

- Learn more about **Past Lives:**

Past Lives

* * *

- Visit **Eckankar.org** to explore a vast array of spiritual resources to aid you in your search for truth.

- Get **books** on a wide variety of spiritual topics at ECKANKAR's books website: **ECKBooks.org**.

- **Call or write us:**
  ECKANKAR
  PO Box 2000
  Chanhassen, MN 55317-2000 USA
  (952) 380-2222

ECKANKAR's
Spiritual Living Courses

Go higher, further, deeper with your spiritual experiences!

ECKANKAR offers enrollment in the Spiritual Living Courses for Self-Discovery and God-Discovery. This dynamic program of inner and outer study unlocks the divine love and wisdom within you. It offers step-by-step advances in enlightenment through spiritual initiations.

From the first day, you can have direct experience with the God Current and begin to meet life's challenges on the highest possible ground.

You will enjoy monthly lessons (also available online) from the spiritual leader of ECKANKAR, Sri Harold Klemp, creative spiritual practices for daily life, and the quarterly *Mystic World* publication. Optional classes with like-hearted Souls are available in many areas.

Here's a sampling of titles from the first course:

- In Soul You Are Free
- Reincarnation—Why You Came to Earth Again
- The Master Principle
- The God Worlds—Where No One Has Gone Before?

ECK courses

Learn more about
ECKANKAR's Spiritual Living Courses.

For Further Reading

By Harold Klemp

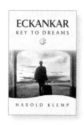

ECKANKAR—Key to Dreams

Unlock the power of your dreams.

Dreams are a spiritual gold mine. They offer glimpses into past lives, soothe a broken heart, and settle the deepest questions in life. But it takes a certain knowledge to reach the inner worlds.

In *ECKANKAR—Key to Dreams*, Sri Harold Klemp, the spiritual leader of ECKANKAR and a leading expert on dreams, shows how anyone can enrich their life through the dynamic art of dreaming.

He offers spiritual exercises to

- recall dreams,
- dream consciously,
- resolve karma, and

- get answers on health, love, finances, and
  more.

Unlock the full potential of your dreams,
and experience a life of greater adventure. Start
your dream study today!

———

ECKANKAR—Key to Soul Travel

Curious about Soul Travel?

One in three Americans reports having had
a remarkable experience—of leaving the physical body or something similar. But how many
have understood the phenomenon?

Have you already experienced the freedom
and joy beyond this physical world? Or are you
just curious? Either way, you can benefit from
reading this book and trying a daily spiritual
practice.

In ECKANKAR—*Key to Soul Travel*, Sri Harold
Klemp—the spiritual leader of ECKANKAR and

foremost authority on Soul Travel—offers spiritual exercises to:

- travel to your inner worlds during sleep,
- understand the meaning of inner experiences, and
- go beyond prayer and astral projection to a high spiritual state of Seeing, Knowing, and Being.

Read this short book to begin your Soul adventure. Taste the divine love and freedom that are your birthright!

To get these and other books to ignite your spiritual life, visit ECKANKAR's page on Amazon via the QR Code below.

ECK books

See ECKANKAR books on Amazon.

Glossary

Words set in SMALL CAPS are defined elsewhere in this glossary.

Blue Light   How the MAHANTA often appears in the inner worlds to the CHELA or seeker.

chela   A spiritual student of ECKANKAR and the LIVING ECK MASTER.

ECK   The Life Force, Holy Spirit, or Audible Life Current which sustains all life.

ECKANKAR *EHK-ahn-kahr*   The Path of Spiritual Freedom. Also known as the Ancient Science of SOUL TRAVEL. A truly spiritual way of life for the individual in modern times. The teachings provide a framework for anyone to explore their own spiritual experiences. Established by PAUL TWITCHELL, the modern-day founder, in 1965. The word means Coworker with God.

ECK Masters   Spiritual Masters who can assist and protect people in their spiritual studies and travels. The ECK Masters are from a long line of God-Realized SOULS who know the responsibility that goes with spiritual freedom.

God-Realization   The state of God Consciousness. Complete and conscious awareness of God. To love as God loves.

Harold Klemp   The present MAHANTA, the LIVING ECK MASTER. SRI Harold Klemp became the MAHANTA, the Living ECK Master in 1981. His spiritual name is WAH Z.

HU   *HYOO*   An ancient, sacred name for God. It is a carrier of love between God and SOUL and can be sung aloud or silently to oneself to align with the God Current. It is the Sound of Soul.

initiations   Steps of enlightenment. The ECK initiation is a sacred ceremony in which the spiritual student is linked to the Sound and Light of God for greater wisdom and love.

Karma, Law of   The Law of Cause and Effect, action and reaction, justice, retribution, and reward, which applies to the lower or psychic worlds: the Physical, Astral, Causal, Mental, and Etheric PLANES.

Living ECK Master   The spiritual leader of ECKANKAR. He leads SOUL back to God. He teaches in the physical world as the Outer Master, in the dream state as the Dream Master, and in the spiritual worlds as the Inner Master. SRI HAROLD KLEMP became the MAHANTA, the Living ECK Master in 1981.

MAHANTA   An expression of the Spirit of God that is always with you. Sometimes seen as a BLUE LIGHT or Blue Star or in the form of the

134

MAHANTA, the LIVING ECK MASTER. The highest state of God Consciousness on earth, only embodied in the Living ECK Master. He is the Living Word.

Paul Twitchell   An American ECK MASTER who brought the modern teachings of ECKANKAR to the world through his writings and lectures. His spiritual name is PEDDAR ZASKQ.

Peddar Zaskq   The spiritual name for PAUL TWITCHELL, the modern-day founder of ECKANKAR and the MAHANTA, the LIVING ECK MASTER from 1965 to 1971.

planes   Levels of existence, such as the Physical, Astral, Causal, Mental, Etheric, and SOUL Planes.

Satsang   A class in which students of ECK discuss a monthly lesson from ECKANKAR.

Self-Realization   SOUL recognition. The entering of Soul into the Soul PLANE and there beholding Itself as pure Spirit. A state of Seeing, Knowing, and Being.

Shariyat-Ki-SUGMAD   Way of the Eternal; the sacred scriptures of ECKANKAR. The scriptures are comprised of twelve volumes in the spiritual worlds. The first two were transcribed from the inner PLANES by PAUL TWITCHELL, modern-day founder of ECKANKAR.

Soul   The True Self, an individual, eternal spark of God. The inner, most sacred part of each person. Soul can see, know, and perceive all things. It is the creative center of Its own world.

Soul Travel   The expansion of consciousness. The ability of SOUL to transcend the physical body and travel into the spiritual worlds of God. Soul Travel is taught only by the LIVING ECK MASTER. It helps people unfold spiritually and can provide proof of the existence of God and life after death.

Sound and Light of ECK   The Holy Spirit. The two aspects through which God appears in the lower worlds. People can experience the Sound and Light by looking and listening within themselves and through SOUL TRAVEL.

Spiritual Exercises of ECK   Daily practices for direct, personal experience with the God Current. Creative techniques using contemplation and the singing of sacred words to bring the higher awareness of SOUL into daily life.

Sri   A title of spiritual respect, similar to reverend or pastor, used for those who have attained the Kingdom of God. In ECKANKAR, it is reserved for the MAHANTA, the LIVING ECK MASTER.

SUGMAD   *SOOG-mahd*   A sacred name for God. It is the source of all life, neither male nor female, the Ocean of Love and Mercy.

Temples of Golden Wisdom   Golden Wisdom Temples found on the various PLANES—from the Physical to the Anami Lok. CHELAS of ECKANKAR visit these temples in the SOUL body to be educated in the divine knowledge. Sections of the SHARIYAT-KI-SUGMAD, the sacred teachings of ECK, are kept at these temples.

Wah Z *WAH zee* The spiritual name of SRI HAROLD KLEMP. It means the secret doctrine. It is his name in the spiritual worlds.

For more explanations of ECKANKAR terms, see *ECKopedia: The ECKANKAR Lexicon,* by Harold Klemp.